Cancer Boo-Boo

Hi! I'm Maddie. Let me share a story about when I was little. It's a true story about when my mommy had cancer.

I've known lots of boo-boos. There's the one I had on my knee from falling off my bike; the boo-boo on my brother's finger from picking his nail; and the blister on my friend's heel from her new pair of shoes.

I'd say, overall, those boo-boos made sense to me.
All of them simply needed a quick hug or a Band-
Aid, and then we could carry on with the day.

There was one boo-boo I didn't understand at first, and this one needed more than just a Band-Aid. This boo-boo was my mommy's breast cancer.

Why do I call her breast cancer a boo-boo? That's how she explained it to my brother and me.

We were little at the time, and I remember her sitting us down on the steps and saying, "Mommy has a boo-boo inside of my boobie." Ha! We laughed at the sound of it, until we remembered boo-boos aren't fun to have.

At first, I was worried and confused. We were good listeners as she told us about how her boo-boo would get better. Mommy said she was going to the hospital for a couple days where the doctor would take out the boo-boo.

She called that having surgery.

The surgery wouldn't hurt because the doctor would put her to sleep. I remembered hoping Mommy didn't snore!

The day came when Mommy had her surgery. When it was over and Mommy woke up, she spent a couple more days at the hospital to rest. Grandma stayed with us while Daddy visited Mommy at the hospital.

When Mommy came home, she was sore where
the boo-boo had been. She had a couple of
Band-Aids on her chest that she had to keep clean.

My brother and I decided we could help Mommy and Daddy by picking up around the house. I got really good at making my own bed, cleaning up my toys, and feeding our dog, Casey.

Mommy was so proud of us! We were happy to have her back home.

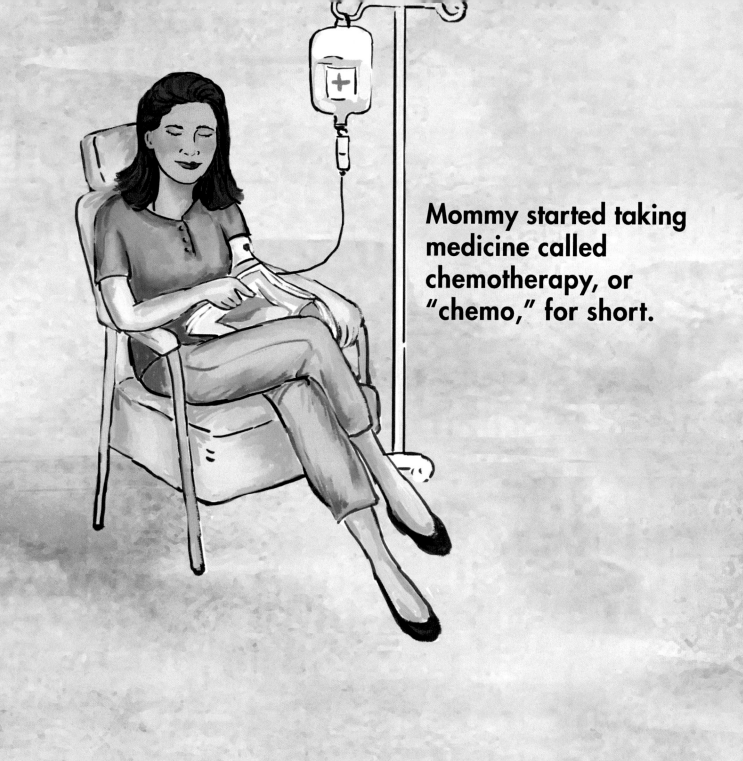

Mommy started taking medicine called chemotherapy, or "chemo," for short.

Mommy had us imagine pieces of cancer as small as specks of sand, tough to see unless you're looking at them under a microscope. The chemo was strong medicine, used to take away those specks.

Chemo was such a strong medicine that it made Mommy's hair fall out! Good thing she warned us ahead of time.

When her hair started coming out, it was **EVERYWHERE.**

Mommy decided it was time to get rid of her hair the fun way, by having a hair-shaving party!

She sat in a lawn chair out back and we each took turns using the clippers.

My brother even gave Mommy a Mohawk! We laughed
a lot, and Mommy did too.

We took pictures that night and stayed up past our bedtimes trying on all of the new hats Mommy was going to wear on her newly shiny, bald head.

Daddy turned on music as we danced around in the hats.
It was so silly seeing my brother wear the fancy hat.

Did I tell you Daddy shaved his head, too? What a pair!

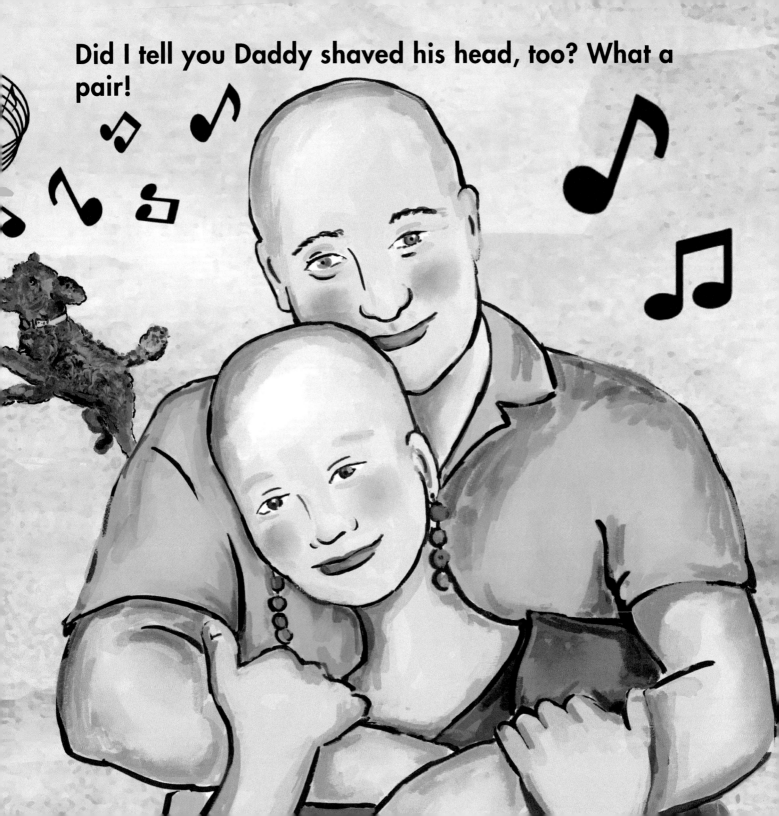

With or without her hair, she was still my mommy and she still looked so beautiful.

Mommy said her medicine would make her a little tired, and it did. She seemed to need more rest every time she went to get chemo. When she napped, Daddy took over.

He made our lunches, took us to the park, and did my hair in some crazy new ways. We realized Daddy makes way bigger bubble baths than Mommy! We loved learning all these fun new things about each other!

When chemo was finally finished, Mommy's hair grew back in a jiffy.

Now that time has passed, she can wear a ponytail again AND she's back to pushing us on the swings at the park!

It took more than a Band-Aid for Mommy's boo-boo to be better, but she did great. We all did great! I'm glad we went through it together.

Cancer boo-boos aren't fun to have, but they don't have to stop you and your family from having fun together!

What about you? Does someone you love have cancer? It's your turn to share about it.

Add *your* story here!

And over here!

A closing note from Maddie:

I hope you enjoyed our story and that you are able to find new ways your family can continue to enjoy family life during cancer treatment.

After my mom's initial diagnosis in 1998, my parents created the Stefanie Spielman Fund for Breast Cancer Research. Since then, the Spielman Fund has raised millions of dollars to support breast cancer research at The James Comprehensive Cancer Center and Solove Research Institute. The Spielman Fund helps us keep our mom's legacy alive every single day. We will not stop until we achieve her goal of a cancer-free world. We will continue to fight and continue to live every day in honor of her.

If you would like to make a donation to the Stefanie Spielman Fund for Breast Cancer Research, scan the link below:

Cover and interior illustrations by:
Donna Stackhouse
Illustration and Graphic Design
https://www.dstackillustration.com/

Publishing Services by Telemachus Press, LLC
7652 Sawmill Road
Suite 304
Dublin, Ohio 43016
http://www.telemachuspress.com

ISBN: 978-1-956867-23-7 (eBook)
ISBN: 978-1-956867-22-0 (Paperback)

Library of Congress Control Number: 2022905465

Version 2022.04.28